Made Simple

PICTURE FRAMING

Sonia Aarons

Bloomsbury Books
London

Page 2:   A grouped assortment of the framer's art.

This edition published in 1994 by Bloomsbury Books,
an imprint of   The Godfrey Cave Group,
42 Bloomsbury Street, London. WC1B 3QJ

Under license from   Harlaxton Publishing Limited
2 Avenue Road, Grantham, Lincolnshire, NG31 6TA, United Kingdom.
A member of the Weldon International Group of Companies.

Copyright © 1994   Harlaxton Publishing Limited
Copyright Design © 1994   Harlaxton Publishing Limited

Publisher: Robin Burgess
Design and Coordination: Rachel Rush
Editing: Martyn Hocking
Illustrator: David Cook, Linden Artists
Photography: Chris Allen, Forum Advertising Limited
Typesetting: Seller's, Grantham
Colour Reproduction: GA Graphics, Stamford
Printing: Imago, Singapore

British Library Cataloguing-in-Publication data.
A catalogue record for this book is available from the British Library.
Title: Made Simple - PICTURE FRAMING
ISBN: 1-85471-372-8

Made Simple

CONTENTS

Everyone has a favourite picture they have been meaning to frame. It could be a family photograph, a tapestry completed after many hours of work, a sketch of your own, a watercolour picked up at a local car boot sale or art exhibition, a poster given for Christmas or simply a picture from a magazine that has caught your eye. Put a frame around it and it is immediately transformed and becomes a focal point.

A framed picture can find a home in any room of the house, even the bathroom or kitchen. Some of the most interesting anecdotes and events from people's lives are recorded on the walls of the downstairs loo! A framed print of your favourite cartoon will cheer you every time you see it; a collection of humourous items grouped together is even better and makes good alternative reading! Rather than pin your children's paintings on the kitchen cabinet, why not frame them for their bedroom?

Picture Framing Made Simple shows you step by step how to make the best of your pictures. From choosing the right style frame and colour mount (the card surround), through to cutting the moulding, mount and glass. For the more ambitious, *Picture Framing Made Simple* shows how to create eye-catching, decorative effects with painted frames and mounts with attractive borders.

Using the right equipment correctly is important if you are to achieve a satisfactory end result. A badly-made frame and poorly-cut mount will immediately detract from the picture, reducing its impact.

Picture Framing Made Simple describes everything you will need to do-it-yourself; types of moulding, glass, mount boards, hanging accessories and how to use the specialised tools like a mount-cutter and mitre-box or saw.

Once you have achieved a simple picture frame and mount you may like to extend your creative talents to specially finished frames, decorated with unusual effects such as tortoiseshelling and marbling. The mounts too can be decorated quite easily and *Picture Framing Made Simple* shows you the various ways this can be done.

Never think your picture is not worth framing, but remember it will benefit from being carefully hung. A single small picture hung too high on a large wall will look lost. While, oddly enough, a large picture on a relatively small wall can look stunning. *Picture Framing Made Simple* will help you make the most of your pictures once they are framed, with ideas for hanging arrangements. So, where did you put that print Auntie gave you for Christmas?

OPPOSITE: Framed pictures can add style and a finishing touch to any room in the home.

Made Simple
GETTING STARTED

F raming does not need a special workshop, just a good size work surface and room to move lengths of moulding and sheets of glass safely.

MAKING ROOM

The dining room table may appear the most convenient, but it really is not always the best place for framing, particularly if it is a small room. Lengths of moulding can be supplied up to 10ft long and if you have to cut this length or even half of it, manoeuvring can be tricky ...... and possibly fateful for anything delicate on the shelf behind you!

You will need to clamp the mitre-box or saw to the surface you are using – a well-polished table would not appreciate it! A kitchen table could be a better choice and you could cover the surface with a piece of chipboard ensuring first that the table is protected by a cloth – an old sheet perhaps. Make sure the board is secure and overlaps the table beneath.

Ideally, choose a room where if need be the moulding can pass through a window or a door; alternatively you could cut the frame roughly to size in a garage or outside. You will also need space to safely handle a large sheet of glass if you are not having it cut to size, as well as room to put all the materials you need conveniently to hand. A shelf or trolley placed close by to hold the equipment you are going to be using is always helpful.

Make sure that you will have room to lay a frame down on the table without it hitting the wall and that the floor can be swept easily (ideally it should be tiled or covered in lino). Sawdust, glue and paint stains are the main hazards.

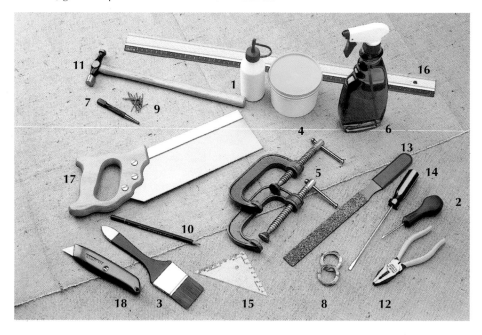

EVERYDAY TOOLS

You will need to gather some basic tools to start with:

1: ADHESIVE – a strong, quick-drying, wood glue for joining corners.

2: BRADAWL – for drilling pilot holes for picture hanging fittings.

3: BRUSH – to keep dust away from the picture and glass.

4: FILLER – for minor repairs.

5: G-CLAMPS – for holding moulding and mitre-box, if used, in place.

6: GLASS CLEANER – to remove stains and finger prints from the glass surface.

7: NAIL PUNCH/SET – for driving in panel pins.

8: NYLON CORD OR PICTURE WIRE – for hanging the frame.

9: PANEL PINS – for pin fastening and joining.

10: PENCIL – a soft pencil for marking.

11: PIN HAMMER – with a suitable size and type of head.

12: PLIERS – for cutting picture framing wire and to remove pins if necessary.

13: RASP – for chamfering rough edges of backboard.

14: SCREWDRIVER – for attaching fittings.

15: SET SQUARE – for checking joints are square.

16: STRAIGHT EDGE – a steel ruler.

17: TENON SAW – which does not whip about as much as a handsaw.

18: TRIMMING KNIFE – a craft knife or similar with snap-off blades.

SPECIAL TOOLS

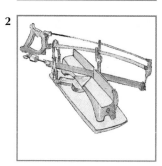

Y ou will also need some items you are unlikely to find in the tool box. Many of the tools for picture framing are simple, inexpensive and easily available.

Some, however, can only be found in art or framing shops and depending on whether you are likely to frame just one picture or a number over a period of time, you will need to decide how much you are prepared to spend.

Mitring Equipment

In particular, there is a choice of mitring equipment. You will need a mitre tool of some description to cut accurate corners for your frames. Nothing ruins the look of a frame more than poorly-cut corners which do not meet and sad to say, even some professional framers are at fault here, simply because they use blunt equipment.

1 The simplest is a mitre-box used with a tenon saw. This has two angled slots into which you place the saw and you can achieve reasonable results as long as the box is held firmly clamped to the work bench and the moulding is also held in place.

2 A larger investment, but well worth it if you intend to make several frames, is a mitre-saw. These are marked with constant cutting angles, normally of 45°, as well as others suitable for making several-sided frames – even hexagons if you get really ambitious!

Mitre-saws will adapt to the depth of the moulding (some will cut wood up to 150mm/6in deep) and have built-in clamps to ensure the moulding is held firmly in place. The saw has a clamp to secure it to the working surface.

Glass-Cutters

A good glass-cutter is essential if you are to attempt cutting your own glass to size. Alternatively, you can ask your dealer to cut the glass once you have the frame and mount ready. The best type of glass-cutter, used by professional framers, has a handle which contains oil. This constantly lubricates the blade and prevents it heating up and becoming blunt, also helping it run more smoothly.

> **Most DIY stores sell a simple glass-cutter, which should be lubricated with cutting-oil or white spirit. These, with a little practice (it is an acquired talent), can achieve good results.**

Clamps

To make up the frame you will need a means of holding the four sides together. To do this you could use four corner clamps or a specially made set of clamps linked by a tape. One corner includes a winding mechanism which allows you to adjust the tape linking all four corners. This means you can clamp all the corners together at once and tighten or loosen the tape according to the size of the frame and the pressure needed.

Staple Guns

Professional framers favour an alternative to hammering in panel or veneer pins to hold the hardboard backing in the frame. They use a gun which shoots diamond or arrow-shaped flat metal tabs into the frame, between the frame and the hardboard backing, to create a picture 'sandwich'.

Made Simple
CHOOSING
A MOULDING

You will probably have to buy your mouldings from an art shop or professional framing shop, although some trade suppliers may be prepared to sell you the odd length.

While there are thousands of wooden mouldings to choose from, metal frames can be supplied cut to size. Metal frames, which can look splendid around modern posters, are now available in a wide variety of colours and finishes, although they tend to be limited in shape. They are put together with special screw fittings so are simpler to make up.

However, there is a far greater variety of wooden frames to suit all types of picture and you will have a good deal of fun making up your mind. Be prepared to spend some time doing this. Bear in mind that you will need to choose the colour of the mount card at the same time, so take your picture with you.

CHECKING THE DEPTH

Mouldings vary in depth. You will need to take care when you choose the frame that the rebate will be able to accommodate your picture, mount, plus the hardboard, plus the glass (if any).

Tapestries and oil paintings can cause particular difficulties if the moulding is not deep enough and you may need to increase the depth of the rebate of the frame with additional wood. However it is not necessary to use glass with oil paintings or with some tapestries.

There are many attractive frames to choose from; pastel colours and light, plain woods are particularly popular in line with today's lighter decor. Bold primary colours as well as black, silver, traditional gold and darker plain wood are also available; increasingly chosen for their simplicity are natural wood mouldings including pine, beech and ash along with plain woods suitable for decoration, of which more later. These can also look stunning when simply limed and polished.

BELOW: A selection of attractive wood and metal mouldings.

COMPLEMENTING THE PICTURE

Embossed designs, both plain wood and gilded, are ideal for complementing traditional landscapes, but try not to combine too elaborate a frame with a fussy or 'busy' picture.

Where possible, choose a shade from the picture which can be highlighted by the frame. What is known as a gold slip may be of use to lighten a darker wooden frame. A slip is a thin strip of wood, usually in gold but available in other shades too, which sits inside the main frame and is sold in lengths which can be mitred just like normal moulding.

On occasions you may find it useful to buy a ready-made 'swept' frame. This is a traditional-style, pre-fabricated gilt frame (also available in plain or stained wood, oak, mahogany and so on) made to standard sizes and particularly suitable for framing oil paintings and mirrors. This type of frame is available in both rectangular and oval shapes.

BUYING MOULDING

You should make allowances when buying moulding for the amount you will lose when cutting a mitre and making a test cut or too. As mentioned earlier, the ends of the moulding may have to be trimmed back before you can use it. Ideally, buy it to the nearest foot or add about 300mm/12in to the final figure.

To work out the final length needed, first measure the length and width of the artwork or the outside of the mount if you are using one. Add 3mm/$\frac{1}{8}$in to each measurement just to ensure the artwork and mount will not be too tight in the frame. Then add the length of each piece, including the allowance, which will give you the measurement of the frame. Then find the width of the moulding, multiply it by eight (for eight mitres) and add this figure to the figure for the perimeter of the framed item. Finally, add on the cutting allowance.

When you choose the moulding, ensure the lengths you buy match as closely as possible; colours can vary as can widths. Also check that the moulding is not bent, damaged or warped in any way.

ABOVE: Examples of 'swept' frames.

HOW TO CUT MOULDINGS

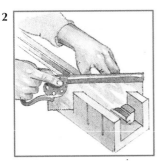

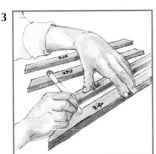

When faced with a 3m/10ft length of moulding (although smaller lengths are available) it is tempting to ask your supplier to cut it up. If possible, avoid doing this; you will inevitably end up with bits of moulding you can not use or which are not quite long enough for what you want.

1 If you are using a mitre-box, hold the wood firmly (it may be helpful to wedge a bit of card under the rebate to make it firm).

2 With the rebate against the far inside of the mitre-box and with the face of the frame upwards, cut the first mitre. You should cut about 50mm/2in from the end of the moulding to make sure you cut the complete angle and to avoid the rough ends of the moulding.

3 Mark each length on the back in pencil as you cut it, 1 and 2 (the longer sides) and 3 and 4 (the shorter sides). Do not try and mark it all in one go – work on one length at a time.

Some woods are softer than others so make sure you saw firmly but without forcing, which may crush the wood. Measure the length of the first leg (cut the longer sides first – you can always cut them down if you make a mistake).

4 Mark the length in pencil on the moulding, measuring along the outside edge, and cut to the pencil line using the appropriate angle and ensuring the back of the moulding is to the far edge of the mitre-box.

5 Once you have cut length 1, you can use this to show exactly where the second mitre should end on length 2. Put the two lengths together so they make a shape like the bow of a ship, and mark the mitre on 2. Cut it in the same way as the first.

6 Repeat the process for 3 and 4 – the two shorter sides.

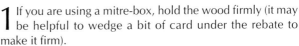

OPPOSITE: Samples of mitred mouldings.

Do not be tempted to sand the rough ends of the mitres, if you do they may not fit together properly. The edges can be smoothed very gently with fine glass-paper wrapped around a sanding-block or you can remove the rough bits with a scalpel or trimming knife. Keep checking that you are not altering the shape, putting the two ends together ensuring they make a neat, clean line – you should hardly see the join (hopefully!) when the frame is finished.

The range of mount boards (or the American term, matts) available will enable you to select a colour, the core (revealed when the bevel is cut) and even the texture of board to suit your picture.

Boards with a black or coloured core instead of the normal white or cream core, can provide a ready-made border when the bevel is cut – often very effective with black-and-white photographs.

You may also wish to decorate the mount, in which case you will need to think about the colour co-ordination of any rules or borders you wish to add.

You can achieve a similar effect by cutting a double mount, using boards in two complementary colours, one cut to give a narrow border inside the other.

Some boards reflect the stippled effects often used as paint techniques, while others have a textured finish rather than being smooth.

If you are framing a valuable picture, a watercolour or sketch, it is advisable to choose a conservation or acid-free board which prevents any discolouration of the picture as the board ages.

You may also cover a mount in fabric or marbled paper, mitring the corners neatly. Ideally, use an adhesive spray which will allow you to move the material or paper around, before it is stuck forever!

SIZING THE PICTURE

It is important before you cut your mount to decide on the size of the window and what area of the picture you want to show. Many pictures benefit from being "cropped" in this way, drawing you into the focal point more immediately.

A photo of a presentation of a trophy, for example, may look far better with just the two people involved shown, rather than a lot of background. It is also a matter of taste; many posters incorporate wording at the bottom, perhaps giving the name of the artist, gallery or exhibition. These often use a large amount of white paper below the picture which some people like, others prefer to be without.

To help you decide on the area, either cut a pair of 'masks' – two L-shaped pieces of card – (ensure they are square), approximately 50mm/2in wide and long enough to accommodate say a picture of 400mm x 500mm/16in x 20in or four straight strips of card so you can build up a "frame". Placing them on the picture will allow you to adjust the size of the window, while framing the area you wish to show. Remember that not all pictures have to be rectangular. Accentuating the narrowness of a picture or its width can create a far more interesting and attractive end result.

OPPOSITE: Sample colour mounts cut as L-shaped 'masks' for sizing the picture with a finished double mount.
NEXT PAGE: A selection of attractive oval cut mounts.

CUTTING THE MOUNT

2

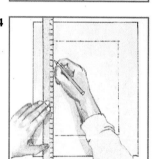

4

Once you have established and noted down the size of the window, you must decide on the width of the border. On average, for balance, 50mm-80mm/2in-3in will be sufficient, although some pictures will lend themselves to wider mounts. Sometimes the smallest picture can look effective in a larger mount, while a large poster may not require one at all.

Cutting the window of the mount is not quite as easy as it looks and it is quite difficult to cut a bevel with a trimming or craft knife. However, it can be done with practice. The ideal tool is a mount-cutter designed for the job which has a blade set at an angle of about 60°. The cutter can also be adjusted for boards of different depths and some include a rule with runner grooves to guide you.

Usually, the top and the sides of the mount are equal and the bottom about a fifth deeper for it to look balanced. For example, the top and the sides could be 60mm/2¾in and the bottom 70mm/3in.

1 Do not presume the mount board is square to start with. Use a set square to check.

2 Cut the board to the size you need with a trimming knife (you do not need a bevel for the outside of the mount).

Cut against a steel rule with its vertical edge, not the bevel edge, against the pencil line.

3 Decide on the width of each border, then add each measurement to the corresponding dimensions of the window and mark the overall width and height of the mount on the back of the board.

You should always mark and cut from the back of the mount board. Rubbing out pencil lines on the face of the board could leave a nasty mark.

4 Mark the dimensions of the window, in pencil. If you are going to cut the bevel with a knife, the type with snap-off blades is best. Beware once you cut the board, the edges can be extremely sharp.

5 The tip of the blade should be placed just to the outside edge of the pencil line so you can see as you cut. Cut against the bevelled side of the steel rule, holding the knife at what you judge to be 60°. The pencil line should be visible on the edge of the cut out window – the centre part.

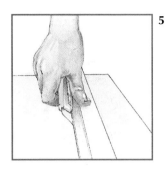

6 Push the tip of the blade into the full depth of the board, starting at the top of the line you are cutting and then, with a tense arm, pull the blade down the length of the line towards your body. Remove the knife cleanly.

7 Turn the board 90° and repeat the procedure for the next cut. You should finish the cut slightly beyond the point where the lines cross each other.

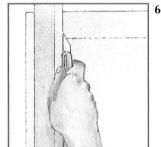

8 When you have made all four cuts, the centre should drop out. It may not always do this immediately, so you will need to re-insert the blade, or use a scalpel very carefully to nick each corner to release the centre cut out. Eventually, you will be able to judge when to stop each cut for the centre to come away cleanly.

Cutting oval or round bevelled mounts is a bit trickier, although if you have a bevel mount cutter it will be somewhat easier. Professionals use a special piece of equipment.

You could, however, use a dish, plate or similar household item as a guide. Use it to make a template and then use this to cut along. You will need to practice to achieve a smooth curve.

You can buy ready-cut oval and circular mounts as well as prepared mounts for framing a number of pictures together – sets of cigarette cards or family snaps.

NEXT PAGE: An attractive selection of completed decorative mounts and frames.

MOUNTING PICTURES

1

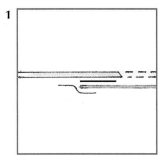

2

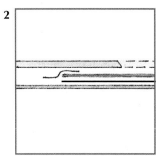

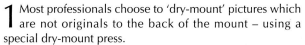

If you want to avoid your pictures wrinkling inside the frame you will need to secure them to a light board in some way. Here are a few variations.

Method One

Dry-mounting uses a special adhesive sheet, sandwiched between the artwork and the mounting card – usually white 1.5mm/^{1}32in card. Specially-treated release paper is used with each sheet to protect the face of the picture from heat.

Always ensure the picture is completely clean and free from dust and grease, or bubbles and tiny dents can appear.

Bonding takes place when the press is at the correct temperature, sealing the artwork and the card together.

Run strips of acid-free tape around the perimeter of the picture attached to the mount for long term strength.

1 Most professionals choose to 'dry-mount' pictures which are not originals to the back of the mount – using a special dry-mount press.

2 Alternatively 'dry-mount' pictures to a separate backing card, then position the mount over the picture.

Method Two

You can utilise the adhesive sheets without a dry-mount press by using a warm iron.

3 Cut the adhesive sheet to the same size as the picture, place it on the back of the picture and, lifting the picture away for a moment, just touch the adhesive sheet in the centre with the warm iron so it is attached to the picture.

4 Place this – with the picture face up in position on the backing card – and once again lightly touch the adhesive sheet with the warm iron to attach it to the card.

Just attach it at one point only as more may cause bubbling.

5 Then place the protective sheet over the picture and iron gently from the centre. Keep the iron very cool to start with, working up to the correct temperature to bond the picture in position.

Dry-mount presses vary in size. Using the smallest – having a 330mm x 400mm/13in x 16in area – it will be necessary to reposition the picture several times to cover the total area.

Method Three

You may also make a hinged mount, using a piece of card the same size as the already cut mount.

6 Trim a piece of card the same size as the cut mount, lay the two together on a flat surface and run a strip of masking tape across the join so that the mount hinges open.

7 Place the picture between the hinged already cut mount and the backing card. Position the picture accurately within the mount window.

8 Ideally use two small pieces of gummed acid-free tape which will not mark the original artwork, sticking them to the back of the artwork so they extend slightly. Then secure these crossways to the backing card with either masking or gummed tape.

Another alternative, is to glue the picture to the backing card. However, beware using an adhesive that is too wet (such as wallpaper paste) which can soak into the picture and cause it to bubble or damage it more severely. 'Spray mount' which comes in a can, is more suitable.

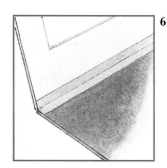

6

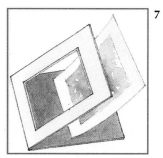

7

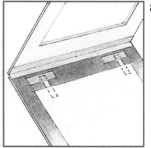

8

BUYING AND CUTTING GLASS

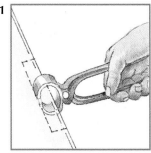

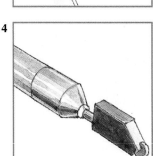

Glass is usually sold in sheets which can be rather awkward to handle and store, but most suppliers will sell cut sheets and will deliver them for you for a charge.

You may prefer to have glass cut to size by a local glass supplier. In that case, measure the area of the frame the picture will drop into exactly and the glass cutter will make the correct allowance for a comfortable fit. Ideally, take the frame, mount and picture with you.

There are several types of glass available, the most widely used being 2mm/¹16in paper float. You may also find an occasional use for non-reflective glass which is more expensive than paper float though it has the unfortunate effect of dulling the picture slightly. Its main advantage is that it enables you to look at the picture instead of yourself if the picture is hung in a brightly lit room.

1 Trying to fit slightly too large a piece of glass into a frame can lead to a nasty accident later if the glass cracks from too much pressure. It is also an awfully fiddly business trimming a slim strip of glass off a piece that has already been cut, although it can be done by nibbling it away with special glass (grozling) pliers.

It is quite easy to cut your own glass once you have the knack although even the experts have their disasters!

2 Ensure you have a flat surface wide enough to take the full size of the sheet of glass – none should extend over the edge or you will be unable to cut correctly.

3 You can only cut glass in complete, straight lines: it is not possible to turn corners in one single cut.

4 You will need a glass cutter, either with a tungsten wheel containing lubricating oil in the handle, to help it to run more smoothly, or a cutter which has to be lubricated by dipping it regularly into a sponge-pad containing cutting oil or white spirit. The latter will not last quite so long and does not have such a good cutting edge.

5 Make sure you have a completely clean surface to work on, perhaps with some cushioning of newspaper or felt under a heavy-card working surface, and mark the size needed on the glass with a fine felt pen or coloured chinagraph (wax) pencil. It is a good idea to practice the technique first on small pieces of glass rather than waste larger pieces.

6 Use a long steel rule to cut against, and ensure the cutter is exactly on the line you have drawn. You will not be cutting right through the glass but merely scoring it.

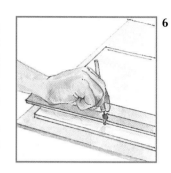

Let the wheel of the cutter run, keeping your fingers straight, pressing firmly and continuously, starting at the top of the line and drawing it down towards you. The pressure should come from your shoulder not the wrist.

You will be able to hear it scoring the surface and the noise should sound fluid rather than crunchy, as the latter would indicate that you are using too much pressure and crushing the glass.

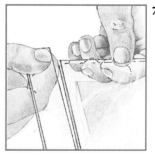

7 The technique now is to break the glass cleanly along the line. Pull the glass over the edge of the table far enough to get a grip with your thumbs, one each side of the cut line.

The thumbs should almost touch each other and your fingers should be underneath the glass. Lift the glass up slightly – half an inch or so – and at the same time, twist your hands away from each other, pushing up with the two fingers under the glass. Watch the glass split – hopefully – down the line.

CUTTING THE BACKBOARD

Probably the easiest task is cutting the hardboard backing. You should use 2mm/^{3}16in hardboard for the backboard, ideally a new type called SBS (smooth both sides) which is half the thickness of ordinary hardboard. Although not generally available, it can be bought from framing suppliers. It can be cut with a trimming knife or a tenon-saw if you find it easier.

Do not try to cut right through with a knife – just score it, then snap it, using a fine rasp or surform to tidy up the edges.

If you cut the hardboard with a saw, smooth the edges down with some sandpaper or again use a fine rasp or surform.

The hardboard backing should fit snugly into the back of the frame and be pinned in as part of the sandwich at the very end of the process. Before doing this, the fittings for the backing should be attached (see page 35).

On some occasions, particularly if the rebate of the frame is shallow, it may be necessary to chamfer the edges and drive the pins or staples into the frame at an angle (see page 31).

You now have the four lengths of mitred moulding, the bevelled mount, the glass, the backboard and the mounted picture.

The next step is to make up the frame. Double check that everything is going to fit within the frame first by making it up as a 'dummy run'.

BELOW: Bring all the elements together for final assembly.

MAKING UP THE FRAME

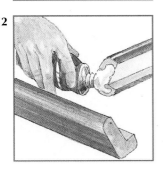

Professional framers use a piece of equipment called an underpinner, which uses air pressure to shoot pins into the frame from the back to reinforce the corners. However, the DIY framer can use panel pins which are hammered into the sides of the frame.

Do not put the pins in from the top or bottom of the frame as the weight of the glass, mount and backing may be too great and may force the frame apart.

You will need two pins at each corner (unless the frame is too narrow and there is only room for one) and it is recommended that you drill the holes for the pins first, using a narrow bit in a hand-drill so that the pin is a tight fit. Only drill the upright leg, not the leg the pin is being driven into.

It is advisable to glue and pin the corners as you go along.

1 Take length 1 (long) and length 3 (short) and check the mitred corners fit neatly together. Pre-drill the holes for the pins in the upright leg and knock the pins in half-way.

2 Smear a touch of wood glue on the two mitred faces. Clamp the first leg in position. Then, putting the two faces together and ensuring the joint is good, clamp the second leg in place. Just wipe off any excess glue that squeezes out.

3 Hit home the pins using a small hammer and, with a nail set, punch them so they disappear just below the surface of the wood. You can fill the resulting dent later with wood filler or wax which can be retouched with matching paint on a very thin brush, or even a water-based, coloured pencil. Leave to set.

4 Do the same with lengths 2 and 4. Then repeat the process with 1 and 4 and 2 and 3.

5 You will need four corner-clamps to hold the corners in the correct position. If you only have one or two clamps, you can do it in stages. To hold the complete frame firmly, use a tape clamp. Ensure this fits straight and holds the frame without twisting. Use the winder which is incorporated in one of the corners to wind the tape so that it holds the corners firmly.

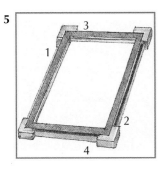

FINAL ASSEMBLY

Having given the frame plenty of time for the glue to set, make sure your working area is clean. The first task is to carefully clean the glass. There is nothing more infuriating than putting together a picture which you then find has a large speck of dust just behind the glass.

1 Rest the glass on a piece of felt or similarly smooth cloth, use a spray glass-cleaner and clean both sides carefully with kitchen roll (it is dust-free, disposable and cheap), ensuring there are no smears.

2 Brush any loose chippings or sawdust out of the rebate of the frame and any specks of dust you can see on the mount or picture itself.

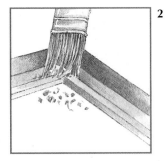

3 Find a shallow box slightly smaller than the overall picture, and arrange the picture and the attached mount and then the glass (taking care to place the glass over the picture directly rather than sliding it across) and the frame on top. Carefully adjust all the elements into the correct position. Turn the whole lot over and place the hardboard backing into the recess.

Use either of two methods to attach hardboard to the frame.

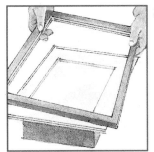

4 Professional framers use a staple-gun which shoots flat metal diamond or arrow-shaped pins into the frame, sandwiching the hardboard to the rest of the picture and holding it all in place.

5 Alternatively you can hammer in fine panel pins. They need to be driven into the inside of the frame with a hammer, so that the length of the pin slides across the backing board, sandwiching it tightly.

Whichever method you use, do not scrimp on pins; use several along each length at regular intervals.

As they are inserted hold a heavy weight (a padded wooden block or lead weight) against the outside edge of the frame to absorb the shock waves.

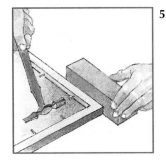

If it is not possible for the backing board to fit flush into the frame, chamfer the edges of the board so that you can drive the pins into the frame at an angle.

THE FINISHING TOUCH

1

Once you have pinned the frame together, there is some tidying up to do and the picture needs to be hung.

1 Cover the pins, holding the back of the frame with strips of either self-adhesive brown paper tape or masking tape, mitring the corners for neatness.

A scalpel is the best way of cutting the tape – just a nick to the corner gives you a nice neat edge. The tape will also help to keep out dust and insects.

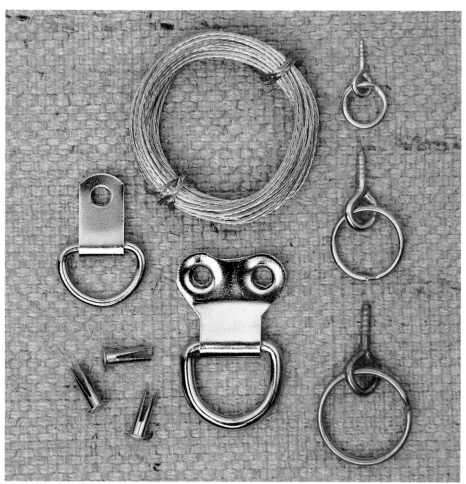

HANGING METHODS

The size of fastenings depends on your picture size. Two screw-eyes and a length of nylon cord will not be adequate to support a large poster but perfectly suitable for a small (250mm x 200mm/10in x 8in) watercolour.

The best type of fittings are D-rings which are rivetted to the backboard about a fifth in from the side of the frame. Alternatively, screw-eyes with a ring for the cord or wire are screwed to the frame, though these may not be suitable for very narrow frames.

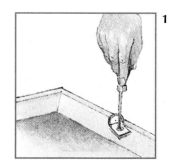

1 Position the fittings about one third of the way down from the top of the picture (D-rings should be fitted to the backboard before you finally assemble the picture) but can also be rivetted to the frame.

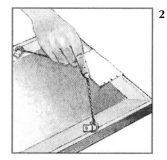

2 Take a length of picture-hanging wire or nylon cord and run it between the D-rings or screw-eyes, allowing a little take-up (not too much) by pushing the wire upward with your finger at the centre point to approximately 50mm/2in from the top of the picture.

3 Tie a double knot through one D-ring and run the wire across to the other D-ring.

4 Return the wire across, twisting the two lengths together to strengthen the cord. Secure the twisted wire through the D-ring at the other end.

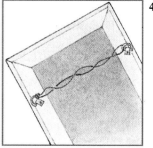

The wall fixing could be as simple as a picture hook or nail, although once again it depends on the size of the picture and to some extent the type of wall. For larger pictures, it is safer to use wallplugs and screws, or use a masonry nail if you are attaching the hook to an outside brick or internal breeze-block wall.

OPPOSITE: A selection of fastenings for hanging.

HANGING PICTURES CREATIVELY

Give some careful thought to displaying your pictures. A small picture hung in the centre of a large wall will look totally lost.

You may feel that the pictures you hang are likely to stay in one place for some time or at least until the room is re-decorated, but it is worth thinking about having the flexibility to change them around or replace them with new ones. Grouping pictures together allows you to do this.

Do not dismiss the more unusual rooms of the house. The bathroom and the loo, the kitchen and the cloakroom, all deserve enlivening and often have unusually-shaped areas where a picture will fit neatly.

However, beware of hanging delicate watercolours or oils in steamy places, such as the bathroom or kitchen. They could be damaged by the humidity.

Other unusual places include over doorways, on the backs of doors, under sloping roofs (as long as it is bright enough) and in recesses alongside chimney breasts.

You can hang a picture alone (if it is striking enough) complemented by the furniture around it – why not place it on an easel, on a mantelpiece or in a recess?

There is no need for a pair of pictures to have exactly the same theme although this works well, of course. If you treat them similarly, with the same frame and mount, they can hang together very well.

No need for them to be hung exactly side-by-side – one a third higher than the other with about a third of the width between them will balance nicely. A table positioned centrally beneath gives more symmetry.

There is no reason either why pictures of different shapes, even ovals, cannot be hung together in a group.

If you take a line as eye level, try and arrange the pictures centred along this line or above and below it. Alternatively you can take an imaginary square, cross or rectangle and build the pictures within this.

Ideally, keep larger pictures at the top of the arrangement and smaller pictures below, where they can be seen more easily.

OPPOSITE ABOVE: A wall covered with pictures can look stunning.
OPPOSITE BELOW: Creative picture hanging on a sloped wall adds interest to a room.

Made Simple

Elizabeth Whiting Associates

Elizabeth Whiting Associates

A few simple but effective framing ideas.

DECORATIVE MOUNTS

There are many ways to decorate a basic mount but you can also add a complementary touch by picking out a colour from your picture in a second mount which slips beneath the main mount to make a slim coloured border.

CUTTING A DOUBLE MOUNT

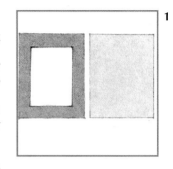

1 Cut the window to fit the picture in the first mount using a coloured card.

2 Select a second piece of card in a complementary colour to the first mount and cut the outside measurements to exactly the same size as the first.

3 Cut out the second mount's window around 5mm/¹4in larger than the first mount. This measurement can vary depending on your taste.

The middle section of the first mount can be dropped onto the marked-out second mount to check that both are square and that the width is equal all the way round.

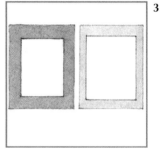

4 Cut out the window of the second mount, then place the frame on top of the first mount.

5 Using double-sided tape, carefully stick the two mounts together to finish the completed double mount.

You can use the same procedure for making a triple mount – perhaps varying the width of the third mount – but ensure the depth of the rebate on the frame will accommodate them all!

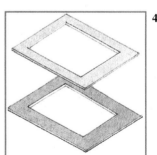

CUTTING A V-GROOVE BORDER

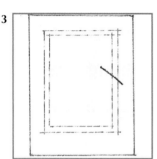

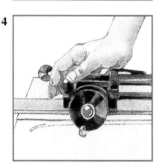

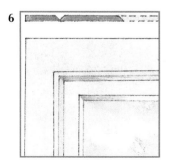

One popular way to decorate a mount is to cut a V-groove. Cut the overall size of the mount card as you would for a single mount.

1 Draw on the back the size you need for the final window – say 50mm/2in at top and sides but 80mm/3in at the bottom.

2 Then draw another rectangle around that, 10mm/^{1}2in (or whatever you decide) closer to the outside edge – 30mm/1^{1}2in at the top and sides and 70mm/2^{1}2in at the bottom.

3 Draw a pencil line on the back from the edge to near the centre so you can replace the cut-out piece the same way up, using the pencil line as a guide for re-positioning.

4 Cut the outside window first to form the cut for the V-groove. Drop the window out, turn it over, face up, and cut the bevel at the same angle as you did from the back. Be careful not to cut too much off.

V-grooves are better cut with the proper hand-tools.

5 Replace the centre piece inside the mount, face down and, making sure the pencil line you drew is aligned on both pieces, then, tape the two together at the back using masking tape.

6 Cut the final window which will frame your picture. The result is the nice effect of a V-groove about 10mm/^{1}2in away from the picture.

DECORATIVE RULES AND BORDERS

Another way of adding a border to a mount is to use a ruling pen filled with gold or other coloured paint.

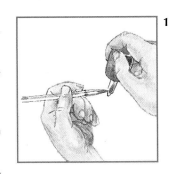

1 Use a pen which allows you to adjust the thickness of the rule and which has a wide nib so it can hold enough ink. Draw your border lightly in pencil before attempting the real thing.

2 You can then fill the borders using water colour wash applied with a sable brush.

If you want to experiment with this technique there is a kit available which uses powder rather than paint and has all you will need to add wash line decoration to your mounts.

The kit includes a corner gauge which enables you to decide where the rules will fall and accurately mark them out (see figure 1, page 42).

BELOW: A sample of mounts with an effective use of rules and borders.

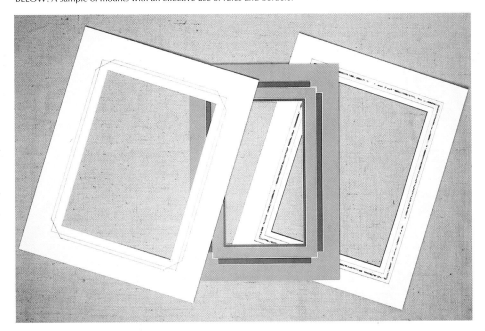

A WASHED LINE MOUNT

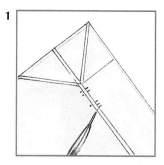

1 Mark an inside and outside ink border, of one or several lines, using a ruling pen and creating a central area which will be filled with colour.

2 Using a straight edge (ruler) draw up the straight lines to link the marked out points.

3 Using an artist's sable brush, load the brush with colour and lightly guide a wet line wash evenly between the marked up lines.

If you are not sure about your drawing ability, there are plenty of other methods of decorating mounts, including mount decoration papers.

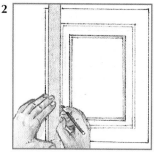

MOUNT DECORATION PAPERS – are thin paper veneers which can be cut from sheets and stuck on with double-sided tape, or supplied with a self-adhesive backing in continuous rolls in a range of designs including marbled, wash and line, antique gold and silver and plain pastels. Corner designs like stencils are also available in this self-adhesive format – or you could use a stencil kit and choose your own colours.

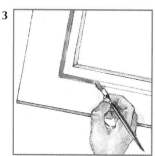

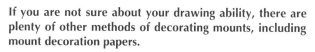

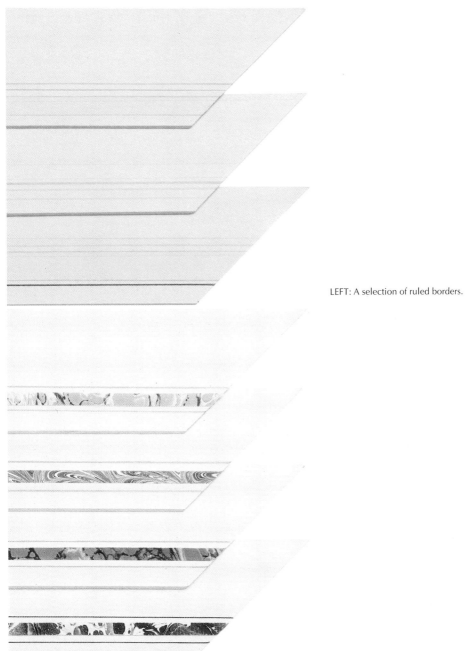

LEFT: A selection of ruled borders.

LEFT: A selection of decorative borders.

DECORATIVE FRAMES

The introduction of plain wood frames has opened up all kinds of possibilities in decorative finishes.

You may wish to show the wood grain off to its full advantage, either staining it with one of the wide range of water or spirit-based wood stain colours that are now available, varnishing it and then brushing on a clear shellac to seal it and give a sheen or gloss finish depending on how many coats you apply.

Alternatively, you can use paint to create some stippled or ragged effects using the same techniques as you would on walls or furniture.

For the more adventurous, it is not so difficult to re-create the effects of marble and tortoiseshell which can look particularly stunning when used to frame mirrors and oil paintings.

It is always helpful to have a sample of the marble or tortoiseshell to hand (or a picture, if the real thing is not available).

You will need:
PLAIN WOOD MOULDING – preferably not too grained or knotty.
UNIVERSAL PRIMER – or sanding sealer.
EGGSHELL PAINT.
WET-AND-DRY SANDPAPER.
ARTIST'S PAINTS.
TIN OF TRANSPARENT GLAZE.
BRUSHES – a selection including fitches, a hog's-hair softening brush, a Japanese Hakka and a small domed-sash or similar brush for tapping on paint.
MASKING TAPE.
ARTIST'S PALETTE – make your own from a piece of hardboard covered in greaseproof paper.

First prepare the frame with the universal primer (or sanding sealer). Build up several layers of eggshell paint (six should do it) and sand it down to a very smooth finish with wet-and-dry sandpaper.

Work on one leg of the frame at a time, masking the mitred corner with masking tape to ensure a clean line.

MARBLING

The two artist's colours we suggest you start with are Payne's grey and raw umber, but you can vary these and add extra colours once you have perfected the technique.

1 Apply a very thin coat of transparent glaze to the first leg of the frame. Then 'tap' on the grey evenly over the entire surface, using the domed-sash or other small brush. Do not make it too dark.

2 Use the hog's-hair softening brush to soften the surface colour – you will be surprised at how marble-like the effect is already.

3 If you do not like the effect in any particular area, just dab it with a rag and soften again with the hog's-hair brush. Then tap in the raw umber along the edges of the grey paint, picking out the shapes that suggest themselves. Skim gently over this with the hog's-hair brush and blend the two colours gently with a fitch brush.

4 To add the veins, use a fine, pointed brush and trickle in the brown (raw umber) paint along routes which suggest themselves, such as the edges of the raw umber. Do not overdo it, but link the veins as you go along.

5 Splatter some white spirit on to the paint with a fitch to create some interesting teardrop effects and colourings.

BELOW: A selection of decorative frames including marbled and limed frames.

TORTOISESHELLING

Y ou can imitate the shell of a turtle (called tortoiseshell) using a similar technique.

1 Apply a thin coat of transparent glaze to the already prepared frame.

2 Mix equal parts of raw sienna and yellow ochre with a touch of glaze.

3 Tap the colour evenly over the prepared frame with a stippling action. Do not make it too thick or the paint will streak when you soften it.

4 Mix some burnt umber with a touch of glaze. Add little dabs to the stippled base with a fitch brush. Imagine you are painting little groups of grains – they should not quite touch each other.

5 A pattern begins to emerge – look out for edges and open spaces similar to those on your sample.

6 Soften the edges with a hog's-hair softening brush, closing up the shapes where they appear.

7 Using the darker raw umber and with a second fitch brush, add highlights where they suggest themselves.

8 Soften the whole with a Hakka which gives a smoother effect than that of the hog's-hair softening brush.

A wide range of other effects can be achieved and training courses are available if this sort of decoration appeals to you. For example, you can re-create malachite, lapis lazuli, birds-eye maple and red leather, to name but a few.

Photographic props supplied by:

Nina Barough Styling

As credited, photographic material reproduced by kind permission of:

Elizabeth Whiting Associates